THE PRACTICAL STRATEGIES SERIES
IN GIFTED EDUCATION

series editors

FRANCES A. KARNES & KRISTEN R. STEPHENS

Independent Study
for Gifted Learners

Susan K. Johnsen & Krystal Goree

PRUFROCK PRESS, INC.

Prufrock Press, Inc.
P.O. Box 8813
Waco, Texas 76714-8813
(800) 998-2208
Fax (800) 240-0333
http://www.prufrock.com

Contents

Series Preface

The Practical Strategies Series in Gifted Education offers teachers, counselors, administrators, parents, and other interested parties with up-to-date instructional techniques and information on a variety of issues pertinent to the field of gifted education. Each guide addresses a focused topic and is written by scholars with authority on the issue. Several guides have been published. Among the titles are:

- *Acceleration Strategies for Teaching Gifted Learners*
- *Curriculum Compacting: An Easy Start to Differentiating for High-Potential Students*
- *Enrichment Opportunities for Gifted Learners*
- *Independent Study for Gifted Learners*
- *Motivating Gifted Students*
- *Questioning Strategies for Teaching the Gifted*
- *Social & Emotional Teaching Strategies*
- *Using Media & Technology With Gifted Students*

For a current listing of available guides within the series, please contact Prufrock Press at (800) 998-2208 or visit http://www.prufrock.com.

Andy was a small, 5-year-old kindergartner. After a short period of time, his teacher realized that he could read fluently on a fifth-grade level and knew most of the math concepts through the fourth grade. She also discovered that Andy enjoyed any books about space travel and astronomy, particularly black holes. His father, a physics professor at a nearby university, would frequently read his textbooks to Andy as bedtime stories.

Mr. Hall, a middle school teacher, is implementing a unit on "change" and wants his students to examine a change that has occurred since their parents were children and then predict what might happen to their children in the same area of change.

John and his friends have formed an astronomy club as part of a mentoring program in their high school. They have identified a mentor at the local community college, raised money to purchase a high-powered telescope, and hold seminars every afternoon for students interested in joining their club.

Each vignette is an example of a situation where independent study and research was effectively implemented. Andy did research on black holes, set up a learning center for the other students in his school so they could learn about his favorite topic, and even initiated and wrote an astronomy column for the school newspaper. All of the students in Mr. Hall's class conducted research, either independently or with others who were interested in the same topic of change. They shared their findings at a "change fair" that included inventions in medicine, flight, education, literary styles, war, and a variety of topics related to their passions. John and his friends conducted research as a foundation for their weekly astronomy seminars and as a requirement for an independent study course their teacher developed to meet state high school requirements.

Independent study is the most frequently recommended instructional strategy in programs for gifted students and is included in the majority of introductory texts as a means for differentiating and individualizing instruction (Clark, 2002; Colangelo & Davis, 2003; Davis & Rimm, 1998; Feldhusen, VanTassel-Baska, & Seeley, 1989; Gallagher & Gallagher, 1994; Parker, 1989; Swassing, 1985; Treffinger, 1986). Independent study is also a preference of gifted students (Dunn & Griggs, 1985; Renzulli, 1977a; Stewart, 1981). When compared to learning styles of more average students, gifted students like instructional strategies that emphasize independence such as independent study and discussion. However, while gifted students like these methods, they do not always have the necessary skills that are essential to self-directed learning; consequently, they need to learn them. Once they have acquired the critical independent strategies, gifted students are able to become lifelong learners, capable of responsible involvement and leadership in a changing world (Betts, 1985).

Johnsen and Johnson (1986b) defined independent study as "the process that you apply when you research a new topic by yourself or with others" (p. 1). Along with the process of research, Kitano and Kirby (1986) added the important elements of planning and teacher involvement: "Students conduct self-directed research projects that are carefully planned with the teacher and are monitored frequently" (p. 114). Both Betts (1985) and Renzulli and Reis (1991) emphasized the importance of "real-world investigations" in their definitions. "In-depth studies are life-like for they provide an opportunity to go beyond the usual time and space restrictions of most school activities" (Betts, p. 55). Type III research projects are "investigative activities and artistic productions in which the learner assumes the role of a first-hand inquirer—thinking, feeling, and acting like a practicing professional" (Renzulli & Reis, p. 131).

In summary, independent study is a planned research process that (a) is self-directed, (b) is similar to one used by a practicing professional or is authentic to the discipline; (c) is facilitated and monitored by the teacher; and (d) focuses on lifelike problems that go beyond the regular class setting.

Models such as Renzulli's Enrichment Triad Model (1977a; Renzulli & Reis, 1997), Feldhusen and Kolloff's (1986) Three-Stage Model, Treffinger's (1975, 1978, 1986) Self-Initiated Learning Model, and Betts and Kercher's (1999) Autonomous Learner Model have inspired teachers to include independent study as an important component of their programs.

Renzulli's (1977a) model contains three qualitatively different phases: Type I enrichment or general exploratory activities introduce the student to a variety of topics and interest areas; Type II group training activities develop creativity and research skills; and Type III investigations encourage students to pursue real problems of personal interest to them (see Figure 1). Students move among and between the three types of activities as based upon their interest in a particular question, topic, or problem. When students arrive at Type III activities, the teacher helps them identify specific questions and methods to use in pursuing their independent studies. The teacher also provides feedback and helps the student find resources and

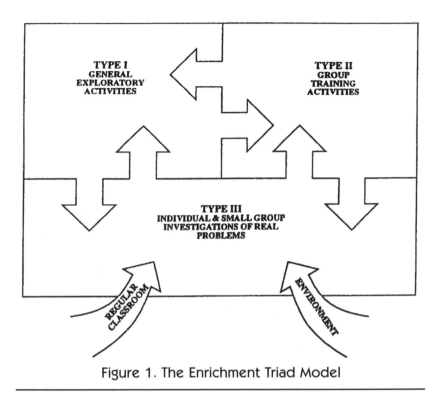

Figure 1. The Enrichment Triad Model

Note. From *The Enrichment Triad Model: A Guide for Developing Defensible Programs for the Gifted and Talented* (p. 14), by J. S. Renzulli, 1977a. Mansfield Center, CT: Creative Learning Press. Copyright ©1977 by Creative Learning Press. Reprinted with permission.

audiences who might be interested in their products (Renzulli, 1979). Renzulli (1979) emphasizes the importance of finding "real" problems and using "authentic" methods during the Type III activities.

Feldhusen and Kolloff's (1986) Purdue Three-Stage Enrichment Model focuses on the development of basic divergent and convergent thinking abilities at Stage 1, more complex creative and problem-solving activities at Stage 2, and independent learning abilities at Stage 3 (see Figure 2). In the independent learning stage, gifted students are involved in research projects that focus on defining problems, gathering data, interpreting findings, and communicating results. At this

Stage I
- **Divergent & Convergent Thinking Abilities**
- Teacher-led short activities
- Emphasis on fluency, flexibility, originality, elaboration
- Application of skills in various content areas
- Balance between verbal and nonverbal activities

Examples of Resources

- *Basic Thinking Skills* (Harnadek, 1976)
- *New Directions in Creativity* (Renzulli & Callahan, 1973)
- *Purdue Creative Thinking Program* (Feldhusen, 1983)
- *Sunflowering* (Stanish, 1977)

Stage II
Development of Creative Problem-Solving Abilities
- Teacher-led and student-initiated
- Techniques of inquiry, SCAMPER, morphological analysis, attribute listing, synectics
- Application of a creative problem-solving model

Examples of Resources

- *CPS For Kids* (Stanish & Eberle, 1996)
- *Problems! Problems! Problems!* (Gourley & Micklus, 1982)
- *Design Yourself!* (Hanks, Belliston, & Edwards, 1977)
- *Hippogriff Feathers* (Stanish, 1981)

Stage III
Development of Independent Learning Abilities
- Student-led, teacher-guided
- Individual or small group work on selected topics
- Application of research methods
- Preparation of culminating product for an audience

Example of Resources

- *Big Book of Independent Study* (Kaplan, Madsen, & Gould, 1976)
- *Self-Starter Kit for Independent Study* (Doherty & Evans, 1980)
- *Up Periscope!* (Dallas Independent Schools, 1977)
- *Interest-A-Lyzer* (Renzulli, 1977b)

Figure 2. The Purdue Three-Stage Model

Note. From "The Purdue Three-Stage Enrichment Model for Gifted Education at the Elementary Level," by J. F. Feldhusen and P. B. Kolloff, 1986, in J. S. Renzulli (Ed.), *Systems and Models for Developing Programs for the Gifted and Talented* (p. 131), Mansfield Center, CT: Creative Learning Press. Copyright ©1986 by Creative Learning Press. Reprinted with permission.

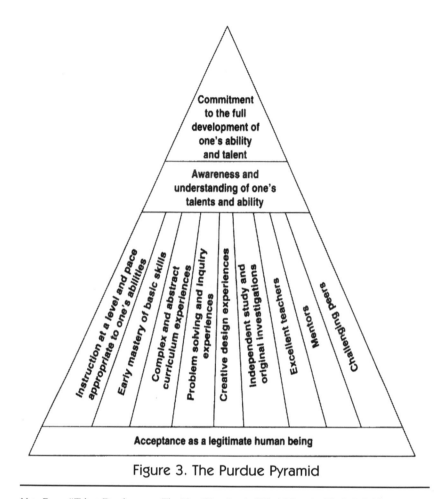

Figure 3. The Purdue Pyramid

Note. From "Talent Development: The New Direction in Gifted Education" by J. F. Feldhusen, 1995, *Roeper Review, 18*, p. 92. Copyright ©1995 by *Roeper Review*, P.O. Box 329, Bloomfield Hills, MI 48303. Reprinted with permission.

stage, the students' own interests and knowledge base serve "to stimulate a deep intrinsic interest in an area of investigation" (p. 131). More recently, Feldhusen (1995) proposed the Purdue Pyramid (see Figure 3). Included in the wide array of learning experiences needed to develop talent and still occupying a prominent position is "independent study and original investigations" (p. 92).

Levels of Self-Direction

Decisions to be made	Teacher-Directed	Self-Directed—Level 1	Self-Directed—Level 2	Self-Directed—Level 3
Goals and objectives	Teacher prescribes for total class or individuals.	Teacher provides choices or options for students.	Teacher involves learner in creating options.	Learner controls choices; teacher provides resources and materials.
Assessments of entry behaviors	Teacher tests, then makes specific prescription.	Teacher diagnoses, then provides several options.	Teacher and learner hold diagnostic conference; tests employed individually if needed.	Learner controls diagnosis; consults teacher for assistance when unclear about some need.
Instructional procedures	Teacher presents content, provides exercises and activities, arranges and supervises practice.	Teacher provides options for student to employ independently at his or her own pace.	Teacher provides resources and options, uses contracts that involve learner in scope, sequence, and pace decisions.	Learner defines project and activities, identifies resources needed, makes scope, sequence, and pace decisions.
Assessment of performance	Teacher implements evaluation procedures, chooses instruments, and gives grades.	Teacher relates evaluation to objectives and gives student opportunity to react or respond.	Peer partners used to provide feedback; teacher and learner conferences used for evaluation.	Learner does self-evaluation.

Figure 4. Treffinger's Model for Self-Directed Learning

Note. From "Teaching for Self-Directed Learning: A Priority for the Gifted and Talented," by D. J. Treffinger, 1975, *Gifted Child Quarterly, 19,* p. 47. Copyright ©1975 by the National Association for the Gifted. Reprinted with permission.

Treffinger (1975) developed a four-step plan for teaching increasing degrees of independent, self-initiated learning (see Figure 4). At the Teacher-Directed Level, the teacher prescribes all the activities for individual students. At Level 1, the teacher creates the learning activities and the student chooses the ones he or she wants to do. At Level 2, the student participates in decisions about the learning activities, goals, and evaluation. And, at Level 3, the student creates the choices, makes the selection, and carries out the activity. The student also evaluates his or her own progress.

More recently, Treffinger (2003) has identified self-directed learning as one "style" that might be observed in a classroom (p. 14; see Figure 5). The emphasis in the student-teacher contract style (i.e., contracting) and self-directed learning style (i.e., exploring) is on student-led or student-managed activities where the teacher acts as a facilitator of independent and group efforts. The other styles are controlled either by the teacher (i.e., command and task styles) or by the group (i.e., peer partner styles).

Betts and Kercher (1999) divided their Autonomous Learner Model into five major dimensions: orientation, individual development, enrichment activities, seminars, and in-depth study (see Figure 6). During orientation, the students learn about themselves and what the program has to offer. In individual development, the student focuses on developing skills, concepts, and attitudes that promote lifelong independent, autonomous learning. Enrichment activities assist students in deciding what they want to study independently. Seminars provide a forum for students in small groups to present their research to the rest of the group. Students learn how to promote understanding of their topics and facilitate the discussions. During the final in-depth study, students pursue areas of interest in long-term individual or small-group studies similar to Renzulli's Type III projects.

While these and other models of independent study exist, empirical research is limited, with most of the studies focusing

Teacher–Directed Styles

Command Style
Emphasis: Directing

The teacher controls decisions about goals and objectives, diagnostics, learning activities, and evaluation. This style is beneficial when the goals emphasize conveying information, teaching specific skills, or communicating basic declarative knowledge and concepts within a prescribed curriculum area. It may be appropriate for "enthusiastic beginners" who need considerable task direction.

Task Style
Emphasis: Enabling

The teacher controls decisions about goals, objectives, diagnostics, and evaluation. The students have some choices regarding learning activities. This style is beneficial when the goals include content at varying levels of difficulty, or varying themes within a broad topic area. It still provides considerable task direction while offering some support for student choices. It is appropriate when the teacher begins teaching the students how to make choices and deal with mobility and freedom of movement.

Group–Directed Styles

Peer Partner Styles with two substyles (Peer teaching and Cooperative)
Emphasis: Collaborating

These styles are highly interactive, as the teacher begins to involve the students in shared decisions about goals and objectives, diagnostics, learning activities, and evaluation.

Peer Teaching or Tutoring. Members of the groups are dissimilar in relation to the task on which they are working. One (who is proficient in relation to the task) serves as the "teacher partner," or tutor, and the other is the "learner partner," for whom the task represents a new and important goal. The students begin to define and carry out the "teacher" role with a peer, before undertaking it for themselves. Cooperative groups. The groups members are relatively similar in relation to the task at hand. The group members work together in planning, carrying out, and evaluation learning activities, after conferencing with the teacher. The major purpose is to serve as a "prelude" for self-direction.

Self–Directed Styles

Student-Teacher Contract Style
Emphasis: Contracting

The student takes increasing control and responsibility for decisions about goals and objectives, diagnostics, and evaluation. Students negotiate specific contracts or learning agreements with the teacher, including all four areas of instructional decisions. There will be specific curriculum relevance or "pay-off" in the contracts; the teacher will involve students in individual and group evaluation, but retains final "approval" and evaluation authority.

Self-Directed Learning Style
Emphasis: Exploring

Individuals, or student-initiated teams pursue projects they have designed. They assume leadership for goals and objectives, diagnosis, activities, and evaluation. They are responsible for demonstrating the appropriateness and relevance of their plans in relation to acceptable educational goals or requirements and for documenting the quality and quantity of their work and results. They may involve outside resources or mentors.

Figure 5. Classroom teaching styles

Note. From *Independent, Self-Directed Learning: 2003 Update* (p. 14), by D. J. Treffinger, 2003, Sarasota, FL: Center for Creative Learning. Copyright ©2003 by Center for Creative Learning. Reprinted with permission.

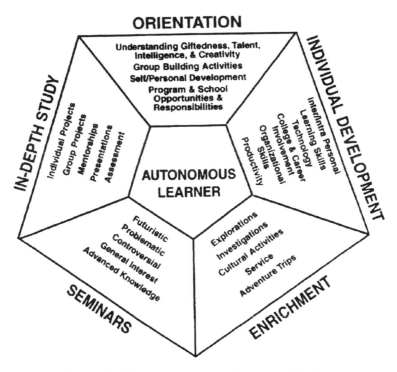

Figure 6. The Autonomous Learner Model

Note. From *The Autonomous Learner Model: Optimizing Ability* (p. 2), by G. T. Betts and J. J. Kercher, 1999, Greeley, CO: ALPS Publications. Copyright ©1996, ALPS Publications. Reprinted with permission.

on Renzulli's model. For example, students who completed Type III investigations reported that they were better prepared for research assignments, "were able to manage their time efficiently, and plan their work to meet their desired goal" (Hébert, 1993, p. 27). They have higher self-efficacy with regard to creative productivity and are more likely to pursue creative productivity outside of school (Starko, 1988). Delcourt (1993) found that students were more internally motivated toward projects they wanted to do and viewed other types of projects such as regular and gifted class assignments as "routine" or "regular" and not a part of creative activities. Olenchak and Renzulli (1989) found that students enrolled in Schoolwide Enrichment

Model (SEM) schools had numerous creative products that exceeded the norm of typical student creative production. Gifted students who have participated in these programs feel that independent study has a positive influence on their motivation and career, their study habits and thinking processes, the degree of challenge, and the opportunity for self-expression in school (Renzulli & Gable, 1976; Zimmerman & Martinez-Pons, 1990).

Using Kuhlthau's Information Search Process Model, Bishop (2000) reported that the most difficult stage in independent study is exploring and forming a focus for the project. This stage appears critical to the success of the process and shows the importance of the teacher's guidance in framing the problem and organizing information.

Implementing the Strategy

In using the strategy of independent study, the teacher may teach all or some of the following steps, depending on the nature of the study and the students' previous experience with conducting research.

Step 1. Introducing the Independent Study

In most cases, the teacher will want to begin by introducing the characteristics of an independent study, providing each student with a plan to manage his or her work (see Figure 1 on p. 8). At this stage, the teacher describes (a) various steps that will be used during the study, (b) the dates when different stages of the study are due, and (c) the audience who will be interested in the results of the study.

Students will be more involved in the independent study if the topic is of genuine interest to them and if they know it will be used or heard by an authentic audience. For example, when a second-grade gifted class was introduced to the problem of limited recycling in their community, they immediately pin-pointed the lack of curbside services as a contributing factor. With the help of their teacher, they identified the city council as an important audience because the members held the budg-etary power to make changes in the current recycling program. Their entire study then focused not only on researching various aspects of recycling, but also on how to sell their ideas to the council. Their enthusiasm and their professional video were rewarded with the desired change. Curbside services indeed improved the recycling program within their community.

Step 2. Selecting a Topic

At this step, the students select a topic to study. It may be a problem they want to solve, an issue they want to debate, an opinion they want to prove, something they want to learn how to do, or simply an area they want to know more about. Interesting ideas may be pursued immediately or collected over a period of time. For example, a bulletin board of expressed classroom opinions might be developed with the purpose of proving or disproving them later. Newspaper headlines can become issues or problems for community action studies. Ideas and new questions that grow from classroom units can be researched immediately or stockpiled for future investigations.

When students have difficulty selecting a single area for study, they may want to consider some of these questions:

- Which topic is most interesting to me?

- Which topic do I know the least about?

- Which topic do I know the most about?

- Which topic will be easy to find information?

- Which topic is the most unusual?

- Which topic will be the most useful to me?

- Which topic will be the most interesting to the audience?

This step frequently involves gathering more information about the topic. Students may investigate by contacting museums, agencies, universities, and state or national departments. They may send letters home to parents, put bulletins that request topic information in the teachers' lounge, interview experts in the field, call public radio and television stations, and, of course, browse through the school library. The teacher may also help by inviting experts to discuss their fields of study with the class, taking the class on field trips, or setting up learning centers that provide an overview of a specific topic. During this process, students may discover they can't locate information about their topic, that the information is too technical or too difficult to understand, that it is really not very interesting to them after all, or that another topic is more appealing. Throughout, the teacher lets the students know that seemingly good ideas don't work and new ideas may appear accidentally or in unusual places. This step is important. If students are energized by their topics, the teacher may assume the role of facilitator, rather than dictator.

For example, Alice happened to be in a fourth-grade resource room with five other gifted children—all of whom were boys. The boys were interested in discovering methods for designing new video games. Alice could care less about games; instead, she was really interested in penguins. While her choice created some difficulty for the teacher who had wanted a group-designed project, she eventually acquiesced to Alice's interest. The result was a beautifully designed zoo for Emperor Penguins.

Step 3: Organizing the Study

Sometimes, the teacher assists students in organizing or "mapping" their topics to help them find specific questions or problems. For example, if the teacher asks the students to brainstorm problems related to space explorations and the result includes only questions about UFOs and aliens, then this step is needed.

Organizational structures may include (a) descriptions, (b) comparisons, (c) causes and effects, or (d) problems and solutions. In *describing* space exploration, for example, the teacher might want to begin by creating categories for brainstorming. These categories may include space exploration's contributions, future, features, history, changes, stages, or people's beliefs, feelings, or criticisms about it. Each of these broader categories forms the hub of a wheel of student ideas and, eventually, questions.

Any of the descriptors generated about space exploration can be *compared* to other topics, models, theories, or rules. For example, the teacher might encourage the students to compare technological and human space exploration; historical and current beliefs about space exploration's contributions to science; or the features of early spacecraft with current or future ones. Again, questions begin to emerge from these comparisons or may lead to other organizational structures such as causes and effects or problems and solutions.

For example, if people have changed their feelings about space exploration, the student may want to consider the *causes and effects* of such a shift in attitudes. What might happen to space exploration's financial support? To scientific advances? To educational benefits? To scientists involved in cosmology? These effects may generate future *problems*. If financial support is withdrawn from space exploration, then the understanding of our solar system and the creation of a broader knowledge base may be limited.

All of these ways of examining a topic should lead to the most important step in the process: asking questions.

Step 4: Asking Questions

After doing some preliminary research and organizing their topics, the students are ready to ask questions. Good questions lead to quality independent studies. Teachers need to teach students the criteria for selecting *good* study questions.

One criterion relates to the question's complexity. Can it be answered by a simple "yes" or "no" or by facts from a reference book? If so, the question may not be one that requires much research. Good study questions often produce several possible answers and may be pursued differently by various researchers. Two other criteria relate to practicality: Does the student have the time or resources to study the question? Is the question useful or beneficial to the student or others? These criteria should help students evaluate their questions.

Students may use their organizational categories to generate questions related to these stems: who, what, when, where, why, how, how much, how many, how long, and how far, along with what might happen if? For example, if a student were studying seals, he or she might ask *descriptive questions,* such as:

- What does a seal look like?

- Where does a seal live?

- When do seals breed?

Or *comparison questions* such as:

- How are seals and penguins alike or different?

- How are the habitats of seals alike or different from other animals?

- How do people feel about seals versus other animals?

Or *cause and effect* questions, such as:

- How do treaties protect seals?

- How have the habitats of seals changed from the past to the present?

- How might habitats change in the future?

Or *problem* questions, such as:

- Why is there a disagreement among countries over the hunting of seals?

- Why is it important to protect species of animals?

- How might the local zoo develop an ideal habitat for seals?

The process of including categories with "W + H" stems should produce a great many questions (e.g., who, what, when, where, why, how, how much, how many, how long, and how far). The teacher might wish to have the student select several questions for study or have the student examine the level of thinking required by each question.

In the latter case, some teachers choose to teach their students a framework for asking questions such as Bloom's taxonomy (Bloom, 1956). In this way, the student can determine the complexity of the question. One approach is to teach them the differences among *little thinking*, *more thinking*, and *most thinking* questions (Johnsen & Johnson, 1986a, p. 19). *Little thinking* (i.e., knowledge and comprehension) questions are those the student can answer by simply copying or redoing something that someone else has done. *More thinking* (i.e., application and analysis) questions are those that can be answered if the student uses the information in new situations. *Most thinking* questions are those that can only be answered if the student creates and evaluates new information. Giving students these evaluation tools helps them create more complex questions that, in turn, influence the overall quality of the independent study.

For example, in Alice's study of Emperor Penguins, she asked several *little thinking* questions such as:

- What are the characteristics of Emperor Penguins?

- Where do they live?

- How do they breed?

- What do they eat?

One *more thinking* question:

- How does the zoo in our city provide a habitat similar to the natural habitat of Emperor Penguins?

And one *most thinking* question:

- What might be an ideal zoo for an Emperor Penguin?

Step 5: Choosing a Study Method

Most of the time, students are aware of only a limited number of methods for gathering information to study a question in an area of interest: the library and, more recently, the Internet. In both cases, students often feel their research is not quite complete without referring to the venerable encyclopedia. This one-type-of-method approach may not even address their study questions. How might Alice answer the question, "How does the zoo in our city provide a habitat similar to the natural habitat of Emperor Penguins?" by gathering information in the library? Alice is going to need to visit the city zoo, talk to the zookeepers, and interview experts who know about Emperor Penguins. In Alice's and other students' studies, the questions should determine the study method.

There are many different kinds of study methods. Some of these methods include descriptive, historical, correlational, developmental, ethnographic, action, experimental, and quasi-experimental research (Issac & Michael, 1995). For example, if students want to know how different schools in their town were named, they would be interested in an historical study method. First, they might contact primary sources such as principals of different schools and people who were either at the school building when it was dedicated or know the person or place for whom/which the school was named. Second, they might locate secondary sources, such as newspaper stories that were written about the people or places for whom/which the schools were named. Third, they would interview their primary sources and take notes from their secondary sources. Fourth, they would review their interviews and notes, focus on facts, and delete biased or exaggerated information. Finally, they would verify information with their primary sources before sharing it with others.

Teachers will want to become acquainted with the research methods that address different kinds of questions so their students will use authentic approaches that are frequently practiced by experts in each field. In addition, teachers will want to engage experts as mentors when students pursue topics in greater depth. What better way to study paleontology than to visit a dig with a practicing archaeologist? To learn about theater with a director of drama? To visit a courtroom with a practicing attorney? Authenticity is supported through the use of scientific methods, experts in various disciplines, a genuine student interest, and multiple approaches to gathering information, which is addressed in the next section.

Step 6: Gathering Information

Both the study method and the information are related to the questions. If a student is interested in the relationship between the number of study hours at home and grades in school, then he or she will use a correlational method of research and gather information from students related to "study hours" and "grades." If students are interested in how an engineer spends his or her time during a workday, they will use a more ethnographic method of research, observing engineers during their workdays.

There are many ways of gathering information. Some of these include note taking, writing letters, surveying, interviewing, observing, reading, listening to focus groups, brainstorming with others, locating information on the Internet, going on field trips, or conducting controlled experiments in a laboratory. In each case, the teacher needs to clearly specify and teach the steps involved with the approach. For example, when interviewing, the student needs to know

- how to select a person to interview;

- how to make the initial contact and set up an appointment;

- how to locate background information and prepare questions for the interview;

- how to make a good impression during the interview;

- how to ask questions and record information;

- how to summarize interview notes; and

- how to provide information to the interviewed person.

With the advent of e-mail, interviews with experts are much more accessible for students. In using the Web, the interested researcher may even take virtual tours of museums all over the world. Again, the teacher plays a valuable role by assisting the student in using search engines, locating reliable sources of information and experts, and critically evaluating the information.

Younger gifted children often gather information through hands-on activities, oral interviews, or surveys. For example, in learning about structures, children might build bridges with various materials, testing the strength of each design by placing toy cars or other objects on top. In deciding what businesses are needed in a classroom "city," they might conduct a "market analysis" through a survey of their classmates.

Remember that gathering information or paraphrasing written materials is a difficult task and should be taught to older students before they begin the process of independent study. In this way, interest in the topic and pacing of the project are not delayed by the frequently perceived "drudgery" of writing notes and outlining information. If students are already proficient in these tasks, then their studies can flow at a rate that maintains their enthusiasm.

In summary, information that is gathered should relate to the question, be authentic within the field of study, be clearly defined and taught to the students, and be appropriate for the age of the researcher.

Step 7: Developing a Product

While most students believe that "independent study" is synonymous with "written report," information may be organized in a variety of ways. Products include books, diagrams, dioramas, videos, computer programs, games, graphs, posters, puppet shows, reports, tape recordings, timelines, debates, dramatizations, models, newspapers, poems, speeches, and many others.

If the product is an option, then students may select one or more to match their original questions. For example, Albert had several questions that related to his topic of interest, "bees." They included "What are the parts of a bee?," "What are the different kinds of bees?," and "Which wild flowers in my neighborhood do bees prefer?" Albert might have answered all of these questions with a written report or a PowerPoint presentation, but he wanted to organize a display for parent open house. To answer the questions related to parts and kinds of bees, he drew a diagram of each one— comparing and contrasting coloration, size, and shape. He mounted these on a poster along with some photos in their natural habitats and labeled each part. For his study question that examined wild flower preferences among bees, he displayed his field notes, presenting the results in a series of graphs. He then prepared an audiotape in which he enthusiastically described the entire process of his independent study.

Similar to the step of gathering information, the product should be authentic within the field of study. For example, what product(s) might a naturalist develop to share his or her work? Did Albert share his bee study in a similar way? Indeed, a naturalist would keep a scientific journal, attach pictures or photos as examples, summarize results in a graph, and present information orally or in written form.

Again, the teacher will want to teach each step of product development. For example, in designing a timeline, the student might

- determine which years will be included;

- decide whether the time line will be horizontal or vertical;

- decide whether to use pictures, drawings, special lettering, or other graphic designs;

- decide the length of the line and each time period;

- draw the line manually or with the computer;

- divide the line into specific time periods;

- write the dates and information beside the time line and attach any pictures or drawings; and

- write a title.

Finally, the way the information is organized should again match the age of the student. Hands-on, visual, and oral products are easier for younger children than written ones. For example, in presenting information gathered about an ancient culture, a class of young gifted students created a museum of artifacts with videos of "experts" describing each display. The teacher will find many resources to help in organizing information into products (see Resources on p. 35).

Step 8: Sharing Information

While information may be shared informally, students need to learn that there is life beyond the product. The teacher might discuss with the students some of these reasons for sharing information: students can learn from one another; students can improve their products; others can help evaluate the product; and students can gather support for the product.

There are two major ways of sharing information with an audience: through oral presentation or in a display. The best approach should be determined by the audience. Again, each step needs to be outlined and taught. For example, in designing an oral report, the student will need to

1. plan the report;

2. practice the report;

3. arrange materials in order;

4. stand in a visible spot;

5. introduce him- or herself;

6. look at the audience;

7. speak loudly enough to be heard;

8. hold the product or visuals where they can be seen;

9. state major points;

10. keep the talk short;

11. ask for questions;

12. have the audience complete the evaluation; and

13. thank the audience.

For an oral report, students should practice before their peers. During these practice sessions, each student should provide at least two positive comments to every one improvement comment that relate to specific criteria. In this way, students' self-esteems and performances will improve.

Sometimes, the process of independent study stops with the completion of a product. Products are graded, taken home, and eventually discarded. For products to *live*, students need to share their ideas, garner support, and develop new ideas that might intensify or create fresh interests in their topics. For example, Albert, who studied bees, might contact entomologists via e-mail or at a local university to discuss the results of his field study. He might improve his techniques through these communications or by actually working with an expert in planning his next study.

Step 9: Evaluating the Study

The evaluation of independent studies is both formative and summative. With formative evaluation, students examine their performance in terms of the overall process. Criteria might include the following statements:

- I had a well-planned independent study.

- I used my time efficiently.

- I wrote a probing study question.

- I used varied resources.

- My research was extensive.

- I developed a fine product.

- My class presentation was effective.

- I have good feelings about the independent study. (Johnsen & Johnson, 1986b, p. 22)

Similar criteria may be developed for other evaluators, such as the teacher, peers, or both. The audience may also contribute their evaluation comments (see Figure 4 on p. 11). All of the evaluations can be collected and reviewed at a final teacher-student conference.

In addition to these types of formative evaluations, the student and teacher will want to use summative evaluation in judging the independent study products. Checklists or rubrics can be designed with specific criteria listed for each type of product. For example, evaluation characteristics for a pictograph might include the following questions:

- Did the pictures relate to the collected data?

- Did the picture reflect the kind of information being expressed? For example, if the graph is about money, money signs ($) or pictures of coins might be used.

- Did each symbol represent the same amount?

- Did partial symbols represent fractions of the amount?

- Were the symbols the same size?

- Were the symbols aligned next to the labels?

- Did the graph have a title that represented the question?

- Was each line of pictographs labeled?

- Was there a key that indicated the amount that each pictograph represented?

- Was the overall graph neat and attractive?

Evaluations in independent studies should focus on what the student has learned and what he or she might do to improve the next research project. If evaluations are positive, the student will be encouraged to continue his or her study, looking for new questions or new areas. There are many evaluations that may be accessed in the literature, such as the Student Product Assessment Form (Renzulli & Reis, 1997), which examines the statement of the purpose; problem focus; level, diversity, and appropriateness of resources; logic, sequence, and transition; action orientation; and audience.

Practical Directions for Using Independent Study

While independent study is frequently used by teachers of gifted students, it is also one of the most abused strategies. Parents often find themselves struggling with their children's September-assigned research projects that are due in the spring. In these cases, teachers provide only grades, with limited instruction and support. In effective independent studies, teachers are actively involved, facilitating each phase of the study as a student's interest emerges and develops. Teachers therefore need to remember the following practical guidelines when initiating independent studies with their students.

Don't confuse ability with skill. While gifted students have a great aptitude for performing at a high level and producing complex products, they may not have the necessary skills for completing an independent study project. For example, they may not know how to identify good study questions, select a sample, use a systematic study method, or gather information from a variety of sources. The teacher will need to teach many of these skills, particularly during the first independent study.

Identify independent study skills. To facilitate the independent study, the teacher must be aware of the skills that are involved in every step of the process. For example, if the student is going to be conducting historical research, the teacher needs to know the specific steps in this method or be able to identify a historian.

Adapt as the student changes. While the teacher needs to have a thorough understanding of the steps in the process, the student's interest *must* guide the study. An interest cannot always be "turned on" according to schedule. Some flexibility must be built into the process so that students have choices of what, when, how, and how much they want to explore a topic.

Use different types of research. "Don't take away my encyclopedia" is quickly being replaced with "Don't take away the Internet!" While both of these are great resources, students also need to learn about firsthand or hands-on research strategies such as interviewing, experimenting, field studies, observing, surveying, discussing, and brainstorming with others. The type of research should match the question and method of study and be authentic to the discipline. For example, if the student is interested in roller coasters, then he or she might study them using the tools of a physicist.

Make it a part of the regular program, not an addition. Sometimes, independent study is something that students do when they finish the rest of their regular work. When this occurs, the student may never have enough time to pursue something of interest, may lose continuity, or, worse yet, may view research as extra work. The teacher may wish to use curriculum compacting to "buy" class time for independent study (Renzulli & Reis, 1997).

Monitor progress and products. Establish a regular time to meet with students, facilitating various phases and stages as they become more involved with their areas of study. This one-on-one time is important to identify needed research skills and to maintain each student's interest.

Develop an appropriate evaluation. The evaluation should match the characteristics of each step in the process and the student's experience with independent study. If the student is pursuing a topic independently for the first time, the teacher should consider this novice-level and evaluate accordingly. Evaluations should improve a student's study skills, encourage his or her interests, and increase a love for learning. If evaluations are too harsh initially, students will quickly lose motivation and follow teacher rules rigidly to receive the desired grade.

Believe in the student's ability and be a model. Nothing is more stimulating to students than others' interest in their independent studies. Teachers should make a point of noticing improvements and new ideas. Teachers who are engaged in their own research provide a model and can discuss their challenges in a collegial fashion with their students.

Remember that independent study is only one way of meeting the needs of gifted students. Sometimes, programs for gifted students are synonymous with independent study because it is the only strategy that is used. Students quickly become bored with a repetition of projects leading to more and more products. Teachers will want to include many different strategies in their programs and limit independent studies to student-driven interests. In this way, students will view independent studies as a gateway to pursuing their passions.

Publications

Betts, G. T., & Kercher, J. K. (2001). *The autonomous learner model: Optimizing ability.* Greeley, CO: ALPS.

This 336-page book is a guide to the Autonomous Learner Model. It describes each of the five dimensions of the model and includes essential activities.

Blair, C. (2003). *Let your fingers do the searching.* Dayton, OH: Pieces of Learning.

This book for grades 7–12 guides students in using 40 reference sources to conduct research. Grading tally sheets and record-keeping assignments are included.

Blandford, E. (1998). *How to write the best research paper ever.* Dayton, OH: Pieces of Learning.

This student workbook for grades 6–12 provides a framework for organizing a well-written research paper. Topics include choosing a subject, works cited, locating and using resources, developing a thesis sentence, outlining, evaluating opposing evidence, and constructing effective conclusions.

Burns, D. E. (1990). *Pathways to investigative skills: Instructional lessons for guiding students from problem finding to final product.* Mansfield Center, CT: Creative Learning Press.

This resource book contains 10 lessons designed to teach students how to initiate a Type III investigation. Lessons focus on interest finding, problem finding, topic webbing, topic focusing, and creative problem solving.

Doherty, E. J. S., & Evans, L. C. (2000). *Self-starter kit for independent study.* Tucson, AZ: Zephyr Press.

This resource book offers tools to guide students through complete independent investigations that target individual interests. It includes ideas for maintaining organized records.

Draze, D. (1986). *Blueprints: A guide for independent study projects.* San Luis Obispo, CA: Dandy Lion.

This book for students in grades 4–8 provides directions for a written report, speech, model, debate, experiment, poster, book, survey, demonstration, learning center, multimedia project, problem solution, science project, game, special event, and display.

Draze, D. (1989). *Project planner: A guide for creating curriculum and independent study projects.* San Luis Obispo, CA: Dandy Lion.

This 48-page book includes suggestions for high-interest topics, hands-on methods of investigation, techniques for processing information, and product ideas that guide teachers and students through project design and independent study.

Heuer, J., Koprowicz, C., & Harris, R. (1980). *M.A.G.I.C. K.I.T.S.* Mansfield Center, CT: Creative Learning Press.

This activity book presents a collection of theme-based activities for Type I and Type II Enrichment experiences.

Johnsen, S. K., & Johnson, K. (1986). *Independent study program.* Waco, TX: Prufrock Press.

This program for students in grades 2–12 includes a teacher's guide with lesson plans for teaching research skills; student workbooks that correlate to the guide and are used for organizing the student's study; and reusable resource cards that cover all the steps of basic research.

Kaplan, S., & Cannon, M. (2001). *Curriculum starter cards: Developing differentiated lessons for gifted students.* Waco, TX: Prufrock Press.

This book includes guidelines for independent study, creative student products, and higher level thinking skills as tools for building units of instruction that emphasize depth and complexity of curricula for gifted students in grades K–12.

Karnes, F. A. & Stephens, K. R. (2000). *The ultimate guide for student product development and evaluation.* Waco, TX: Prufrock Press.

This book offers a step-by-step introduction to using creative projects in your classroom. Ideas for integrating projects into your existing curriculum; ways to help students plan and create their projects; and easy, effective evaluation strategies are provided.

Kramer, S. (1987). *How to think like a scientist.* New York: Crowell.

This book teaches students in grades 2–5 the steps in the scientific method: asking a question, collecting data/information, forming a hypothesis, testing the hypothesis, and reporting the results.

Laase, L., & Clemmons, J. (1998). *Helping students write the best research reports ever.* New York: Scholastic.

This book contains mini-lessons that help students select meaningful topics, navigate references, take effective notes, paraphrase, organize materials, and write research reports that verify learning. Creative product ideas are also included.

Leimbach, J. (1986). *Primarily research.* San Luis Obispo, CA: Dandy Lion.

This 64-page book includes eight units for primary-age children. Each unit presents a different animal or pair of animals and includes interesting facts and activities for structuring research.

Leimbach, J., & Riggs, P. (1992). *Primarily reference skills.* San Luis Obispo, CA: Dandy Lion.

This 64-page book helps students in grades 2–4 learn how to use the library. Reproducible worksheets teach the parts of a book, alphabetical order, dictionaries, encyclopedias, and how to find books.

Lester, J. D., & Lester, J. D. (1992). *The research paper handbook.* Mansfield Center, CT: Creative Learning Press.

This book for students in grades 7–12 targets the writing process, from selecting a topic, to writing a polished paper.

Examples and models that illustrate how to examine various subjects and sources, as well as tips on using computer searches and databases, are included.

Meriwether, N. W. (1997). *12 easy steps to successful research papers.* Mansfield Center, CT: Creative Learning Press.

This resource for grades 7–12 guides students through the process of writing a research paper, from choosing a subject and taking notes, to organizing the structure of the paper and preparing the final copy.

Merritt, D. (2003). *Independent study.* Dayton, OH: Pieces of Learning.

This book for grades 4–12 provides students with tools for planning studies, researching topics, presenting information, and assessing learning experiences. An overview to guide teachers in using the tools to design independent study experiences for students is included.

Mueller, M. (2002). *Great research projects step by step.* Portland, ME: Walch.

This book, which is recommended for grades 7–12, presents research as a thorough process that involves steps including topic selection, finding what students need to know, navigating systems that will help provide needed information, and conducting meaningful research.

Nottage, C., & Morse, V. (2000). *Independent investigation method: Teacher manual.* Mansfield Center, CT: Creative Learning Press.

This manual for teachers working with children in grades K–8 provides instructions for two skill levels, reproducible work-pages and assessment tools, sample research studies, and teacher resource pages. A poster set (sold separately) reinforces the vocabulary and flow of the process.

Polette, N. (1984). *The research book for gifted programs, K–8.* Dayton, OH: Pieces of Learning.

This 176-page book provides more than 150 projects for primary, middle, and upper grades. Critical thinking skills are stressed.

Polette, N. (1991). *Research without copying for grades 3–6.* Dayton, OH: Pieces of Learning.

This 48-page book describes practical approaches for reporting on topics in diverse ways. Different types of research are illustrated along with models.

Polette, N. (1997). *Research reports that knock your teacher's socks off!* Dayton, OH: Pieces of Learning.

This book for grades 3–8 gives specific models and examples to show students different ways to organize information about animals, people, places, and events.

Polette, N. (1998). *The research project book.* Dayton, OH: Pieces of Learning.

This book for grades 4–9 presents more than 100 models for reporting research in divergent ways. The text focuses on models designed to stimulate analysis of information.

Redman, L. T. (2002). *Choosing and charting: Helping students select, map out, and embark on independent projects.* Mansfield Center, CT: Creative Learning Press.

This book for grades 3–6 guides students step-by-step through the process of choosing a topic, finding information, taking and keeping track of notes, conducting interviews, developing appropriate products, and deciding on an audience for presentation. Guidelines and forms to help teachers assess and understand student interests and learning are included.

Renzulli, J. S., & Reis, S. M. (1997). *The schoolwide enrichment model: A how-to guide for educational excellence.* Mansfield Center, CT: Creative Learning Press.

This resource book includes a collection of useful instruments, checklists, charts, taxonomies, assessment tools, forms, and planning guides to organize, implement, maintain, and evaluate different aspects of the SEM in grades K–12.

Roets, L. (1994). *Student projects: Ideas and plans.* Mansfield Center, CT: Creative Learning Press.

More than 250 pages of project and independent investigation ideas are covered in this book on independent study and research for grades 3–12. The text includes models of outstanding student work.

Rothlein, L., & Menbach, A. (1988). *Take ten . . . steps to successful research.* Mansfield Center, CT: Creative Learning Press.

Appropriate for grades 5–8, this book presents the research process in 10 logical steps that include choosing the subject, selecting suitable reference materials, writing an outline, and writing the final copy.

Wishau, J. (1985). *Investigator.* San Luis Obispo, CA: Dandy Lion.

This step-by-step guide for students in grades 4–7 includes

activities in completing and presenting an in-depth research project. Specific information is provided for using the library, selecting a research topic, writing a business letter, writing a biography, conducting an interview, taking a survey, and making a speech.

Woolley, S. (1992). *Writing winning reports.* San Luis Obispo, CA: Dandy Lion.

This set of guides for students in grades 4–7 includes instructions about how to write reports on specific topics such as animals, planets, countries, and explorers. Point breakdowns for grading are also included.

Web Sites

These Web sites will provide teachers and students with information about independent study topics.

Best Environmental Resources Directories
http://www.ulb.ac.be/ceese/meta/cds.html

This site highlights timely topics and publications that focus on environmental and energy issues in society.

iLoveLanguages: Your Guide to Languages on the Web
http://www.june29.com/HLP

This page is a catalog of language-related Internet resources. You may find online language lessons, translating dictionaries, native literature, translation services, software, language schools, or language information.

Internet Resources for Children & Educators
http://www.monroe.lib.in.us/~lchampel/childnet.html

Many references and resources are easily accessed through this Web site, which is sponsored by the Children on the Internet Conference. The Library of Congress, NASA, the National Science Foundation, and the University of California–Berkeley Museum of Paleontology are among the host sites that are linked to this page and provide valuable research information.

KidsOLR: Kids' Online Resources
http://www.kidsolr.com

Numerous resources are provided on this page, including links to information sources that focus on discipline areas such as art, music, geography, history, language arts, math, science, and health.

Kids Web: The Digital Library for K–12 Students
http://www.npac.syr.edu/textbook/kidsweb

This Web site is simple to navigate and contains information at the K–12 level. Categories include the arts, sciences, social studies, miscellaneous, and other digital libraries.

The Math Forum
http://forum.swarthmore.edu

This forum contains math resources organized by subject. Broad topics include numbers, chaos, cellular automata, combinatorics, fractals, statistics, and topology. When exploring numbers, you will find Archimedes' constant, Devlin's angle, Pi, favorite mathematical constants, and many other interesting topics that will link to other sites.

Martindale's The Reference Desk
http://www.martindalecenter.com

Great science discoveries are included among the thousands of science links at this page. ExtraSolar planets, genome mapping, genetic testing, global ecosystem, and top quark may become interesting topics for students interested in science.

Ivy's Search Engine Resources for Kids
http://www.ivyjoy.com/rayne/kidssearch.html

This page offers links to more than 10 search engines and more than 80 Web sites that are appropriate for children and young adults. Research sources are presented according to search engines, Web guides, and specialized searches for kids.

History/Social Studies for K–12 Teachers
http://home.comcast.net/~dboals1/boals.html

The major purpose of this site is to encourage the use of the Internet as a tool for learning and teaching and to help teachers locate and use resources. A wide selection of topics are included under the general headings of archaeology, genealogy, humanities, economics, history, government, research, critical thinking, and more.

ThinkQuest
http://www.thinkquest.org/programs.html

This page provides an opportunity for students and educators to work collaboratively in teams to learn as they create Web-based learning materials and share research.

WWW Virtual Library: Museums Around the World
http://www.comlab.ox.ac.uk/archive/other/museums/world.html

This site provides a comprehensive directory of online museums and museum-related resources. Museums are organized by country and by exhibitions. The USA link also lists the 57 top museum Web sites.

Yahoo!
http://www.yahoo.com

You may search for specific topics using this page or use the listed resources to help you find information. Listed resources relate to arts and humanities, business and economy, computers and Internet, education, entertainment, government, health, news and media, recreation and sports, reference, regional, science, social science, and culture.

Yahooligans!
http://www.yahooligans.com

A search engine designed especially for elementary children. Sites include around the world, art and entertainment, computers and games, school bell, science and nature, and sports and recreation.

References

Betts, G. T. (1985). *The autonomous learner model for gifted and talented.* Greeley, CO: ALPS.

Betts, G. T., & Kercher, J. K. (1999). *The autonomous learner model: Optimizing ability.* Greeley, CO: ALPS.

Bishop, K. (2000). The research processes of gifted students: A case study. *Gifted Child Quarterly, 44,* 54–64.

Bloom, B. S. (Ed.). (1956). *Taxonomy of education objectives: The classification of educational goals. Handbook I: Cognitive domain.* New York: Longmans Green.

Clark, B. (2002). *Growing up gifted: Developing the potential of children at home and at school* (6th ed.). Upper Saddle River, NJ: Prentice Hall.

Colangelo, N., & Davis, G. A. (Eds.)(2003). *Handbook of gifted education* (3rd ed.). Needham Heights, MA: Allyn and Bacon.

Dallas Independent School District. (1977). *Up periscope! Research activities for the academically talented student.* Dallas, TX: Author.

Davis, G. A., & Rimm, S. B. (1998). *Education of the gifted and talented* (4th ed.). Needham Heights, MA: Allyn and Bacon.

Delcourt, M. A. B. (1993). Creative productivity among secondary school students: Combining energy, interest, and imagination. *Gifted Child Quarterly, 37,* 23–31.

Doherty, E. J., & Evans, L. C. (1980). *Self-starter kit for independent study.* Austin, TX: Special Education Associates.

Dunn, R., & Griggs, S. (1985). Teaching and counseling gifted students with their learning style preferences: Two case studies. *G/C/T, 14,* 40–43.

Feldhusen, J. F. (1995). Talent development: The new direction in gifted education. *Roeper Review, 18,* 92.

Feldhusen, J. F., & Kolloff, P. B. (1986). The Purdue three-stage enrichment model for gifted education at the elementary level. In J. S. Renzulli (Ed.), *Systems and models for developing programs for the gifted and talented* (pp. 126–152). Mansfield Center, CT: Creative Learning Press.

Feldhusen, J. F., VanTassel-Baska, J., & Seeley, K. R. (1989). *Excellence in education of the gifted.* Denver: Love.

Gallagher, J. J., & Gallagher, S. A. (1994). *Teaching the gifted child* (4th ed.). Boston: Allyn and Bacon.

Gourley, T. J., & Micklus, C. S. (1982). *Problems! Problems! Problems!* Glassboro, NJ: Creative Competitions.

Harnadek, A. (1976). *Basic thinking skills: Critical thinking.* Pacific Grove, CA: Midwest.

Hébert, T. P. (1993). Reflections at graduation: The long-term impact of elementary school experiences in creative productivity. *Roeper Review, 16,* 22–28.

Issac, S., & Michael, W. (1995). *Handbook in research and evaluation: A collection of principles, methods, and strategies useful in the planning, design, and evaluation of studies in education and the behavioral sciences* (3rd ed.). San Diego, CA: Edits.

Johnsen, S. K., & Johnson, K. (1986a). *Independent study program.* Waco, TX: Prufrock Press.

Johnsen, S. K., & Johnson, K. (1986b). *Independent study program student booklet.* Waco, TX: Prufrock Press.

Kaplan, S., Madsen, S., & Gould, B. (1976). *The big book of independent study*. Santa Monica, CA: Goodyear.

Kitano, M., & Kirby, D. F. (1986). *Gifted education: A comprehensive view*. Boston: Little, Brown.

Olenchak, F. R., & Renzulli, J. S. (1989). The effectiveness of the schoolwide enrichment model on selected aspects of elementary school change. *Gifted Child Quarterly, 33,* 36–46.

Parker, J. P. (1989). *Instructional strategies for teaching the gifted*. Boston: Allyn and Bacon.

Renzulli, J. S. (1977a). *The enrichment triad model: A guide for developing defensible programs for the gifted and talented*. Mansfield Center, CT: Creative Learning Press.

Renzulli, J. S. (1977b). *The Interest-a-lyzer*. Mansfield Center, CT: Creative Learning Press.

Renzulli, J. S. (1979). The enrichment triad model: A guide for developing defensible programs for the gifted and talented. In J. C. Gowan, J. Khatena, & E. P. Torrance (Eds.), *Educating the ablest: A book of readings on the education of gifted children* (2nd ed., pp. 11–127). Itasca, IL: Peacock.

Renzulli, J. S., & Callahan, C. (1973). *New directions in creativity: Mark 3*. Mansfield Center, CT: Creative Learning Press.

Renzulli, J. S., & Gable, R. K. (1976). A factorial study of the attitudes of gifted students toward independent study. *Gifted Child Quarterly, 20,* 91–99.

Renzulli, J. S., & Reis, S. M. (1991). The schoolwide enrichment model: A comprehensive plan for the development of creative productivity. In N. Colangelo & G. A. Davis (Eds.), *Handbook of gifted education* (pp. 111–141). Needham Heights, MA: Allyn and Bacon.

Renzulli, J. S., & Reis, S. M. (1997). *The schoolwide enrichment model: A how-to guide for educational excellence* (2nd ed.). Mansfield Center, CT: Creative Learning Press.

Stanish, B. (1977). *Sunflowering*. Carthage, IL: Good Apple.

Stanish, B. (1981). *Hippogriff feathers*. Carthage, IL: Good Apple.

Stanish, B., & Eberle, B. (1996). *CPS for kids*. Waco, TX: Prufrock Press.

Starko, A. J. (1988). Effects of the revolving door identification model on creative productivity and self-efficacy. *Gifted Child Quarterly, 32,* 291–297.

Stewart, E. D. (1981). Learning styles among gifted/talented students: Instructional techniques preferences. *Exceptional Children, 48,* 134–138.

Swassing, R. H. (1985). *Teaching gifted children and adolescents.* Columbus, OH: Merrill.

Treffinger, D. (1975). Teaching for self-directed learning: A priority for the gifted and talented, *Gifted Child Quarterly, 19,* 46–49.

Treffinger, D. (1978). Guidelines for encouraging independence and self-direction among gifted students. *Journal of Creative Behavior, 12*(1), 14–20.

Treffinger, D. (1986). Fostering effective, independent learning through individualized programming. In J. S. Renzulli (Ed.), *Systems and models for developing programs for the gifted and talented* (pp. 429–460). Mansfield Center, CT: Creative Learning Press.

Treffinger, D. (2003). *Independent, self-directed learning: 2003 update.* Sarasota, FL: Center for Creative Learning.

Zimmerman, B. J., & Martinez-Pons, M. (1990). Student differences in self-regulated learning: Relating grade, sex, and giftedness to self-efficacy and strategy use. *Journal of Educational Psychology, 82,* 51–59.

About the Authors

Susan K. Johnsen is a professor in the Department of Educational Psychology at Baylor University. She directs and teaches courses in the area of gifted education at the undergraduate and graduate levels. She is the editor of *Gifted Child Today* and serves on the editorial boards of *Gifted Child Quarterly* and *The Journal for Secondary Gifted Education*. She is the coauthor of the Independent Study Program and three tests that are used in identifying gifted students: Test of Mathematical Abilities for Gifted Students (TOMAGS), Test of Nonverbal Intelligence (TONI-3), and the Screening Assessment for Gifted Students (SAGES-2). She has published numerous articles and is a frequent presenter at state, national, and international conferences. She is past-president of the Texas Association for Gifted and Talented and serves on the board of The Association for the Gifted (a division of the Council for Exceptional Children).

Krystal K. Goree is director of clinical practice and teaches classes in gifted and talented education at Baylor University. She has worked in the field of gifted education for more than 15 years in the roles of parent, teacher, consultant, presenter, and program administrator. She currently serves on several state committees and provides consultation and program evaluation for school districts. In addition to presenting at state and national conferences, she has authored articles and book chapters. She is past-president of the Texas Association for the Gifted and Talented and serves as senior editor of *Gifted Child Today*.